Grilled Cheese

Sandwich

Cookbook

Introduction

A grilled cheese sandwich is a very American food loved the world over.

Although the idea of putting bread and cheese together has been around since ancient times, the grilled cheese we know and love was thought to have originated in the United States during the 1920's.

Although the idea of putting bread and cheese together has been around since ancient times, the grilled cheese we know and love was thought to have originated in the United States during the 1920's.
In France, the Croque Monsieur (toasted bread, cheese, and ham) was first on menus in 1910.

The term "grilled cheese" doesn't make an appearance in print until the 1960s; before that it was always "toasted cheese" or "melted cheese" sandwiches.

Of course, many different cheeses and breads can be used, as well as different spices and fillers. Meats, veggies and condiments are often added, such as ham, tomato or pickles.

There are many different ways to make a grilled cheese sandwich and this cookbook has a wide variety of recipes to try.

Classic Cheddar Grilled Cheese Sandwich

Ingredients:

2 slices Cheddar cheese
2 slices country white bread
1 tbsp. salted butter plus more if needed

Directions:

1. Heat butter in a cast-iron or nonstick skillet over medium-low heat.
2. Place the cheese between the bread slices.
3. Press the sandwich slightly and place it in the skillet.
4. Cook until golden on the bottom, 3 to 5 minutes.
5. Flip, adding more butter to the pan if needed.
6. Cook until the other side is golden and the cheese melts, 3 to 5 more minutes.

Classic Swiss Grilled Cheese Sandwich

Ingredients:

2 slices Swiss cheese
2 slices country white bread
1 tbsp. salted butter plus more if needed

Directions:

1. Heat butter in a cast-iron or nonstick skillet over medium-low heat.
2. Place the cheese between the bread slices.
3. Press the sandwich slightly and place it in the skillet.
4. Cook until golden on the bottom, 3 to 5 minutes.
5. Flip, adding more butter to the pan if needed.
6. Cook until the other side is golden and the cheese melts, 3 to 5 more minutes.

Classic Monterey jack Grilled Cheese Sandwich

Ingredients:

2 slices Monterey jack cheese
2 slices country white bread
1 tbsp. salted butter plus more if needed

Directions:

1. Heat butter in a cast-iron or nonstick skillet over medium-low heat.
2. Place the cheese between the bread slices.
3. Press the sandwich slightly and place it in the skillet.
4. Cook until golden on the bottom, 3 to 5 minutes.
5. Flip, adding more butter to the pan if needed.
6. Cook until the other side is golden and the cheese melts, 3 to 5 more minutes.

Herb and Cheddar Grilled Cheese

Ingredients:

1 tbsp. butter, softened
2 slices bread
2 slices sharp Cheddar cheese
1 tbsp. chopped parsley
1 tsp. chopped basil
1 tsp. oregano
1 tsp. chopped fresh rosemary
1 tsp. chopped fresh dill

Directions:

1. Spread 1/2 tbsp. of butter on one side of each piece of bread. Lie the slices of Cheddar on one of the slices of bread on the unbuttered side.
2. Sprinkle the parsley, basil, oregano, rosemary, and dill on the other slice of bread on its unbuttered side.
3. Sandwich the two slices of bread together with the buttered sides facing outwards.
4. Heat a skillet over medium heat.
5. When skillet is hot, gently lie the sandwich in the skillet; cook on each side for 3 minutes until cheese has melted.

Mozzarella Cheddar Grilled Cheese

Ingredients:

1 slice sharp Cheddar cheese
1 slice mozzarella cheese
2 thick bread slices
1 pinch dried oregano, or to taste
1 pinch salt and ground black pepper to taste
2 tbsps. salted butter, at room temperature
1 tbsp. chopped fresh parsley, or to taste
1 tsp. chopped fresh chives, or to taste

Directions:

1. Assemble the sandwich by placing Cheddar and mozzarella cheese on the bread.
2. Season with oregano, salt, and pepper.
3. Heat butter in a pan over medium-low heat.
4. Add sandwich and cook until cheeses melt, 3 to 5 minutes, increasing heat if needed.
5. Flip and cook until golden brown, 3 to 5 minutes more.
6. Cut in half and top with parsley and chives.
7. Preheat the oven to 350 degrees F (175 degrees C).
8. Grease a 9x13-inch baking pan.
9. Mix flour, sugar, milk, eggs, baking powder, vanilla, and salt for cake together in a large bowl until completely combined.
10. Slowly pour in butter and mix to incorporate; pour into the prepared baking pan.
11. Whisk brown sugar, flour, and cinnamon for topping together in a bowl.
12. Cut in butter with 2 knives or a pastry blender until well combined.
13. Drop evenly over the batter, then swirl with a knife.
14. Bake in the preheated oven until a toothpick inserted into the center comes out clean, 30 to 40 minutes.
15. Mix powdered sugar, milk, and vanilla for glaze together in a small bowl. Drizzle over the warm cake.

Spicy Grilled Cheese Sandwich

Ingredients:

2 tbsps. butter or margarine
4 slices white bread
2 slices American cheese
1 roma (plum) tomato, thinly sliced
1/4 small onion, chopped
1 jalapeno pepper, chopped

Directions:

1. Heat a large skillet over low heat.
2. Spread butter or margarine onto one side of two slices of bread.
3. Place both pieces buttered side down in the skillet.
4. Lay a slice of cheese on each one, and top with slices of tomato, onion and jalapeno.
5. Butter one side of the remaining slices of bread, and place on top buttered side up.
6. When the bottom of the sandwiches are toasted, flip and fry until brown on the other side.

Jalapeno Popper Grilled Cheese Sandwich

Ingredients:

2 oz. cream cheese, softened
1 tbsp. sour cream
10 pickled jalapeno pepper slices, or to taste - chopped
2 ciabatta sandwich rolls
4 tsps. butter
8 tortilla chips, crushed
1/2 cup shredded Colby-Monterey Jack cheese

Directions:

1. Combine the cream cheese, sour cream, and pickled jalapeno in a small bowl.
2. Set aside.
3. Preheat skillet over medium heat.
4. Slice each roll in half horizontally, then slice the rounded tops off the ciabatta rolls to make a flat top half.
5. Spread 1 tsp. butter on the doughy cut side of the bottom bun and 1 tsp. butter on the now flattened top bun.
6. Place half of the cream cheese mixture, half of the crushed chips, and half of the shredded cheese on the non-buttered side of the bottom bun.
7. Place the top half of the bun on the sandwich and place the sandwich on the hot skillet.
8. Repeat with the second sandwich.
9. Grill until lightly browned and flip over, about 3 to 5 minutes; continue grilling until cheese is melted and the second side is golden brown.

Three-Cheese and Basil Grilled Cheese Sandwich

Ingredients:

1 tsp. mayonnaise
2 slices bread
1 slice jalapeno Jack cheese
1 roma tomato, thinly sliced
1 slice mozzarella cheese
4 leaves fresh basil, chiffonade (rolled and cut into ribbons)
1 slice Cheddar cheese

Directions:

1. Heat a cast iron or nonstick skillet over medium heat.
2. Spread 1/2 tsp. mayonnaise on each slice of bread.
3. Place bread slices mayo-side down in the hot skillet.
4. Place jalapeno Jack cheese on 1 slice of bread, and top with tomato slices.
5. Place mozzarella cheese on the other slice, top with basil, then top with Cheddar cheese.
6. Cook until bread turns golden brown, 3 to 5 minutes.
7. Carefully invert the piece with the tomato onto the piece with the basil.

Sweet Grilled Cheese

Ingredients:

2 slices white bread
2 slices American cheese
2 tsps. brown sugar
2 tsps. softened butter

Directions:

1. Heat a skillet over medium heat.
2. Spread butter onto one side of a piece of bread and place butter side down in the skillet.
3. Place one piece of cheese on top of the bread, then sprinkle with brown sugar.
4. Top with the other slice of cheese.
5. Butter the other slice of bread and place on top with the butter side up.
6. Fry on each side until golden brown, 3 to 5 minutes per side.

Egg in a Hole French Toast Grilled Cheese

Batter Ingredients:

3/4 cup half-and-half
1 large egg
1 tbsp. white sugar
1/2 tsp. ground cinnamon
1/2 tsp. kosher salt

Sandwiches Ingredients:

4 thin slices white sandwich bread
2 slices American cheese
2 slices Cheddar cheese
2 slices cooked bacon, crumbled
1 tbsp. unsalted butter
2 large eggs

Directions:

1. Whisk half-and-half, 1 egg, sugar, cinnamon, and salt together in a bowl until batter is smooth.
2. Place 2 bread slices on a work surface and top each with 1 slice American cheese, 1 slice Cheddar cheese, and crumbled bacon.
3. Top each with a second piece of bread, making a sandwich.
4. Cut a 2-inch hole in the center of each sandwich using a biscuit cutter or 2-inch wide glass.
5. Melt butter in a large nonstick skillet over medium-low heat, tilting the skillet to cover entire surface with butter.
6. Dip both sandwich rings and cut-out holes in the batter until evenly coated.
7. Place the dipped sandwich rings and cut-out holes in the melted butter in the skillet.
8. Immediately crack an egg into the hole of each ring.
9. Cook until egg white is set, bread is golden brown, and cheese is softly melted, about 2 minutes per side.

Grilled Cheese De Mayo

Ingredients:

1 tbsp. mayonnaise, divided
2 slices white bread
2 slices American cheese
1 slice pepperjack cheese

Directions:

1. Spread 1/2 the mayonnaise onto one side of a slice of bread and place, mayonnaise-side down, in a skillet.
2. Place American cheese and pepperjack cheese on top of the bread.
3. Spread remaining mayonnaise onto one side of the remaining bread and place, mayonnaise-side up, on top of the cheese.
4. Cook sandwich in the skillet over medium heat until cheese melts and the bread is golden brown, about 2 1/2 minutes per side.

Pico De Gallo Grilled Cheese Sandwich

Pico de Gallo Ingredients:

1 tomato, diced
1/2 white onion, diced
2 tbsps. chopped fresh cilantro, or to taste
1/2 lime, juiced
salt and ground black pepper to taste

Sandwich Ingredients:

3 tbsps. softened butter, or as needed
10 slices white bread
10 slices provolone cheese

Directions:

1. Mix tomato, onion, cilantro, lime juice, salt, and pepper together in a bowl.
2. Spread butter onto 1 side of each bread slice.
3. Arrange bread, butter-side down, onto a work surface.
4. Place 1 slice provolone cheese onto each bread slice and spoon pico de gallo onto 5 of the bread-cheese slices.
5. Top each pico de gallo layer with remaining bread-cheese slices, butter-side up.
6. Heat a skillet over medium heat.
7. Grill each sandwich in the hot skillet until golden brown and cheese is melted, 3 to 4 minutes per side.

Four-Cheese Grilled Cheese Sandwich

Ingredients:

2 tbsps. salted butter, softened
1 tsp. minced garlic
2 thick slices Italian bread
1 1/2 tbsps. olive oil, divided, or more as needed
2 cups chopped fresh spinach
1/2 cup giardiniera, drained
2 slices mozzarella cheese
2 slices provolone cheese
2 slices Asiago cheese
2 slices Fontina cheese
3 slices Roma tomato, cut lengthwise, or more to taste

Directions:

1. Mix butter and garlic in a small bowl until well combined.
2. Spread 1/2 of the butter onto one side of each slice of bread; set aside.
3. Heat 1 tbsp. oil in a large skillet over medium-low heat; stir in spinach and giardiniera. Sauté until spinach is wilted and mixture is heated through, 3 to 5 minutes.
4. Remove to a bowl and wipe out the skillet.
5. Place 1 slice of bread, buttered-side down, into one side of the warm skillet.
6. Heat 1/2 tbsp. oil in the other side of the skillet.
7. Place mozzarella slices in the skillet and cook until soft, 1 to 2 minutes.
8. Place mozzarella slices on top of the bread in the skillet.
9. Repeat with the provolone, Asiago, and Fontina slices.
10. Add spinach mixture and tomato slices to the skillet, adding more oil if necessary, and cook until warm, 2 to 3 minutes.
11. Place spinach mixture on top of the cheese, followed by the tomatoes and the remaining slice of bread, buttered-side up. Flip the sandwich and cook until browned and cheese has melted, 5 to 10 minutes.

Grilled Cheese and Scrambled Egg Sandwich

Ingredients:

1 large egg
2 tbsps. milk
1/2 tsp. salt
1/2 tsp. onion powder
1/2 tsp. garlic-pepper seasoning
⅓ cup Cheddar-Jack cheese
cooking spray
2 tsps. butter, softened
2 slices bread
⅓ cup shredded mozzarella cheese, or more to taste

Directions:

1. Whisk egg, milk, salt, onion powder, and garlic-pepper seasoning together in a bowl until well combined and pale yellow in color.
2. Dump in Cheddar-Jack cheese and stir until thick.
3. Spray a skillet with cooking spray and set over medium-low heat.
4. Pour egg mixture into the skillet; cook and stir until eggs are set, about 5 minutes.
5. Remove to a plate.
6. Lightly butter one side of each bread slice.
7. Spray the skillet again with cooking spray.
8. Put one slice of bread, buttered-side down, in the pan.
9. Top with 1/2 of the mozzarella cheese, the egg mixture, the remaining mozzarella, and the remaining bread, buttered-side up.
10. Cook until bread is toasted and browned, 1 to 2 minutes.
11. Flip and cook until the other side is browned and the cheese is melted, another 1 to 2 minutes.
12. Transfer to a plate and let cool for a minute before serving.

Roasted Cauliflower Grilled Cheese

Ingredients:

1 small head cauliflower
1/4 cup olive oil
1/2 stick unsalted butter
ground black pepper to taste
2 slices Gouda cheese
2 slices sharp Cheddar cheese
2 slices beefsteak tomato

Directions:

1. Preheat the oven to 425 degrees F (220 degrees C).
2. Line a baking sheet with parchment paper.
3. Remove the tough bottom leaves from the cauliflower, taking care not to remove the stem.
4. Place on a cutting board with the stem facing upwards; cut vertically on both sides of the stem to remove the loose florets. Reserve florets for another use.
5. Cut vertically through the stem into 2 even "steaks", about 1 inch thick.
6. Transfer to the prepared baking sheet.
7. Roast cauliflower in the preheated oven until soft and browned, about 15 minutes.
8. Heat olive oil and butter in a large frying pan.
9. Cook cauliflower until browned on one side, 2 to 3 minutes. Flip cauliflower and shift to one side of the pan so you have space to warm cheese slices.
10. Lay cheese slices in the pan until they begin to melt, then place over the cauliflower steaks.
11. Warm tomato slices in the same way.
12. Season with black pepper.
13. Cover cheeses and tomatoes with the second steak. Flip "sandwich" and cook over low heat until cheeses are melted, 2 to 3 minutes more.

Pesto Grilled Cheese Sandwich

Ingredients:

2 slices white bread
1 slice provolone
1 slice mozzarella
1 tbsp. salted butter plus more if needed
Directions:
1. Heat butter in a cast-iron or nonstick skillet over medium-low heat.
2. Spread pesto on 1 slice white bread.
3. Top with provolone and mozzarella.
4. Top with another slice of bread and cook, flipping once, until golden.

Tomato Pesto Grilled Cheese Sandwich

Ingredients:

2 slices Italian bread
1 tbsp. softened butter, divided
1 tbsp. prepared pesto sauce, divided
1 slice provolone cheese
2 slices tomato
1 slice American cheese

Directions:

1. Spread one side of a slice of bread with butter, and place it, buttered side down, into a nonstick skillet over medium heat.
2. Spread the top of the bread slice in the skillet with half the pesto sauce, and place a slice of provolone cheese, the tomato slices, and the slice of American cheese onto the pesto.
3. Spread remaining pesto sauce on one side of the second slice of bread, and place the bread slice, pesto side down, onto the sandwich.
4. Butter the top side of the sandwich.
5. Gently fry the sandwich, flipping once, until both sides of the bread are golden brown and the cheese has melted, about 5 minutes per side.

Italian Grilled Cheese Sandwiches

Ingredients:

1/4 cup unsalted butter
1/8 tsp. garlic powder
12 slices white bread
1 tsp. dried oregano
1 (8 oz.) package shredded mozzarella cheese
1 (24 oz.) jar vodka marinara sauce

Directions:

1. Preheat your oven's broiler.
2. Place 6 slices of bread onto a baking sheet.
3. Spread a small handful of the mozzarella cheese over each slice.
4. Top with the remaining 6 slices of bread.
5. Mix together the butter and garlic powder, brush some over the tops of the sandwiches, or spread with the back of a tbsp..
6. Sprinkle with dried oregano.
7. Place baking sheet under the broiler for 2 to 3 minutes, until golden brown.
8. Remove pan from oven, flip sandwiches, and brush the other sides with butter, and sprinkle with oregano. Return to the broiler, and cook until golden, about 2 minutes.
9. Cut sandwiches in half diagonally, and serve immediately with vodka sauce on the side for dipping.

Bacon, Tomato & Triple Cheese Grilled Cheese

Ingredients:

1/2 pound smoked bacon
1/2 pound bacon
4 slices sourdough bread
1 (8 oz.) bottle sandwich spread
1/4 pound provolone cheese, sliced
1/4 pound cheddar cheese, sliced
1 pound gouda cheese, sliced
4 slices tomato

Directions:

1. Cook bacon and chicken bacon as required.
2. Start with 2 slices of sourdough bread.
3. Squirt both pieces with the sandwich spread.
4. Layer 2 oz. provolone cheese, 2 oz. peppadew cheese and 2 oz. Smoked Gouda Cheese onto bread.
5. Add 4 slices either bacon or chicken bacon and 2 tomato slices per sandwich.
6. Top with second slice of bread.
7. Can be cooked on a griddle or in a panini press.
8. Cook just until the cheese starts to melt.
9. Serve warm.

Waffle Iron Grilled Cheese Sandwiches

Ingredients:

2 tbsps. mayonnaise
2 tsps. Dijon mustard
4 slices whole-grain bread
2 oz. shredded pepperjack cheese

Directions:

1. Preheat a waffle iron according to manufacturer's instructions.
2. Mix mayonnaise and Dijon mustard together in a bowl; spread onto 1 side of each bread slice.
3. Sprinkle pepperjack cheese over mayo-mustard layer of 2 bread slices.
4. Cover cheese layer with a second bread slice, creating 2 whole sandwiches.
5. Place 1 sandwich in the waffle iron, taking care not to push down all the way. Wait until the bread begins to soften from the heat before starting to gently close the waffle iron, about 2 minutes. Apply more pressure to the top part of the iron, eventually closing it after a total of 3 to 4 minutes.
6. Cook until browned, 2 to 3 minutes more.
7. Repeat with the remaining sandwich.

Pulled Pork Grilled Cheese

BBQ Sauce Ingredients:

2 tbsps. butter
1 medium yellow onion, diced
1 jalapeno chile pepper, diced
1 cup ketchup
1/2 cup brown sugar
Liquid smoke, to taste

Sandwich Ingredients:

1 (3 pound) pork shoulder roast
1 (1 pound) loaf sourdough bread, sliced
16 slices sharp cheddar
4 tbsps. butter

Directions:

1. Melt butter in a medium-size skillet over medium heat.
2. Sauté onions until soft; stir in jalapeños, ketchup, sugar and liquid smoke.
3. Bring to a boil then reduce heat to medium-low and simmer for an hour or until sauce has thickened to desired consistency.
4. Smoke pork shoulder in a hot smoker for 3 to 5 hours at 210 degrees F (internal meat temperature of 150 degrees F).
5. Remove, and wrap in aluminum foil.
6. Refrigerate overnight.
7. Remove excess fat from pork.
8. Using two forks, shred remaining meat into a large bowl.
9. Mix in barbecue sauce.
10. Brown 2 slices of buttered sourdough bread in a skillet or griddle over medium heat.
11. Place a slice of cheese on each slice.
12. Top with pulled pork mixture, a second slice of cheese and another slice of bread. Turn sandwich over when bottom slice has browned and brown the other side.

Bacon and Tomato Grilled Cheese Sandwich

Ingredients:

2 slices cheddar cheese
2 slices country white bread
1 tbsp. salted butter plus more if needed
3 slices crisp bacon
1 slice tomato between

Directions:

1. Heat butter in a cast-iron or nonstick skillet over medium-low heat.
2. Place the cheese between the bread slices.
3. Add bacon and tomato between the cheese.
4. Press the sandwich slightly and place it in the skillet.
5. Cook until golden on the bottom, 3 to 5 minutes.
6. Flip, adding more butter to the pan if needed.
7. Cook until the other side is golden and the cheese melts, 3 to 5 more minutes.

Triple Cheese Grilled Cheese Sandwich

Ingredients:

1 slice cheddar
1 slice muenster
1 slice Swiss cheese
2 slices country white bread
1 tbsp. salted butter plus more if needed

Directions:

1. Heat butter in a cast-iron or nonstick skillet over medium-low heat.
2. Place cheese between the bread slices.
3. Press the sandwich slightly and place it in the skillet.
4. Cook until golden on the bottom, 3 to 5 minutes.
5. Flip, adding more butter to the pan if needed.
6. Cook until the other side is golden and the cheese melts, 3 to 5 more minutes.

Spicy Nacho Grilled Cheese Sandwich

Ingredients:

1 slice Monterey jack or American cheese
1 slice cheddar
2 slices white bread
1 tbsp. salted butter plus more if needed
some pickled jalapeño slices
1 tbsp. salted butter plus more if needed

Directions:

1. Heat butter in a cast-iron or nonstick skillet over medium-low heat.
2. Place the cheese between the bread slices.
3. Place jalapeño slices between the cheese.
4. Press the sandwich slightly and place it in the skillet.
5. Cook until golden on the bottom, 3 to 5 minutes.
6. Flip, adding more butter to the pan if needed.
7. Cook until the other side is golden and the cheese melts, 3 to 5 more minutes.

Crunchy Nacho Grilled Cheese Sandwich

Ingredients:

1 slice Monterey jack or American cheese
1 slice cheddar
2 slices white bread
1 tbsp. salted butter plus more if needed
Some pickled jalapeño slices
1 tbsp. crushed corn chips
1 tbsp. salted butter plus more if needed

Directions:

1. Heat butter in a cast-iron or nonstick skillet over medium-low heat.
2. Place the cheese between the bread slices.
3. Place jalapeño slices between the cheese.
4. Add crushed corn chips.
5. Press the sandwich slightly and place it in the skillet.
6. Cook until golden on the bottom, 3 to 5 minutes.
7. Flip, adding more butter to the pan if needed.
8. Cook until the other side is golden and the cheese melts, 3 to 5 more minutes.

Goat Cheese–Peppadew Grilled Cheese Sandwich

Ingredients:

1/2 cup cream cheese
1/4 cup goat cheese
8 chopped Peppadew peppers
2 slices multigrain bread
1 tbsp. salted butter plus more if needed

Directions:

1. Mix cream cheese, goat cheese and peppers.
2. Sandwich one-quarter of the mixture between bread.
3. Heat butter in a cast-iron or nonstick skillet over medium-low heat.
4. Cook, flipping once, until golden.

Diner Sandwich Grilled Cheese Sandwich

Ingredients:

2 slices American cheese
2 slices white bread
Mayonnaise
Ketchup for serving
1 tbsp. salted butter plus more if needed

Directions:

1. Heat butter in a cast-iron or nonstick skillet over medium-low heat.
2. Place 2 cheese between white bread.
3. Spread mayonnaise on the outside of the sandwich and cook, flipping once, until golden.
4. Serve with ketchup.

Cheddar and Pickles Grilled Cheese Sandwich

Ingredients:

2 slices aged white cheddar cheese
2 slices white bread
Sliced pickles
Mayonnaise
Ketchup for serving
1 tbsp. salted butter plus more if needed

Directions:

1. Heat butter in a cast-iron or nonstick skillet over medium-low heat.
2. Place cheese between white bread.
3. Place sliced pickles between the cheese.
4. Spread mayonnaise on the outside of the sandwich and cook, flipping once, until golden.
5. Serve with ketchup.

Garlic Grilled Ham and Cheese

Ingredients:

2 thick slices frozen garlic bread
2 slices Monterey jack
2 slices ham
1 tbsp. salted butter plus more if needed

Directions:

1. Prepare garlic bread as the label directs.
2. Heat butter in a cast-iron or nonstick skillet over medium-low heat.
3. Sandwich with Monterey jack and ham.
4. Cook, flipping once, until golden.

Avocado Grilled Cheese

Ingredients:

1/4 sliced avocado
Lime juice to taste
Lime zest to taste
2 slices white bread
2 slices pepper jack cheese
1 tbsp. salted butter plus more if needed

Directions:

1. Toss avocado with lime juice and lime zest to taste.
2. Sandwich pepper jack and avocado between slices of bread.
3. Heat butter in a cast-iron or nonstick skillet over medium-low heat.
4. Cook, flipping once, until golden.

Potato Chip Grilled Cheese

Ingredients:

Yellow mustard
2 slices whole-wheat bread
2 slices American cheese
8 potato chips
1 tbsp. salted butter plus more if needed

Directions:

1. Spread mustard on 1 slice bread.
2. Top with cheese and potato chips.
3. Top with another slice of bread.
4. Heat butter in a cast-iron or nonstick skillet over medium-low heat.
5. Cook, flipping once, until golden.

Artichoke Grilled Cheese on Rye

Ingredients:

2 tbsps. grapeseed oil
1/2 red onion, thinly sliced
8 slices German rye bread
salt and ground black pepper to taste
4 slices smoked Gouda cheese
4 slices provolone cheese
1/4 cup marinated artichoke hearts, drained and chopped

Directions:

1. Heat grapeseed oil in a large skillet over medium heat.
2. Sauté onion until softened and slightly browned, 5 to 10 minutes.
3. Transfer onion to a small bowl, reserving the oil in the skillet.
4. Lightly brush each bread slice with grapeseed oil from the skillet and season with salt and pepper.
5. Arrange half the bread slices, oil-side down, in the skillet.
6. Top each bread slice with 1 slice Gouda cheese, 1 slice provolone cheese, artichoke hearts, and onion; top with remaining bread slices, oil-side up.
7. Cook sandwiches until bread is browned and crispy and cheeses are melted, about 4 minutes per side.
8. Slice each sandwich in half to serve.

Swiss Mushroom Grilled Cheese

Ingredients:

2 slices rye bread
Thousand Island dressing
2 slice Swiss cheese
Sautéed mushrooms and onions
1 tbsp. salted butter plus more if needed

Directions:

1. Heat butter in a cast-iron or nonstick skillet over medium-low heat.
2. Spread rye bread with Thousand Island dressing.
3. Sandwich with 1 slice Swiss cheese, some sautéed mushrooms and onions, and another slice of Swiss.
4. Cook, flipping once, until golden.

Four-Cheese Grilled Cheese Sandwich

Ingredients:

2 tbsps. salted butter, softened
1 tsp. minced garlic
2 thick slices Italian bread
1 1/2 tbsps. olive oil, divided, or more as needed
2 cups chopped fresh spinach
1/2 cup giardiniera, drained
2 slices mozzarella cheese
2 slices provolone cheese
2 slices Asiago cheese
2 slices Fontina cheese
3 slices Roma tomato, cut lengthwise, or more to taste

Directions:

1. Mix butter and garlic in a small bowl until well combined.
2. Spread 1/2 of the butter onto one side of each slice of bread; set aside.
3. Heat 1 tbsp. oil in a large skillet over medium-low heat; stir in spinach and giardiniera. Sauté until spinach is wilted and mixture is heated through, 3 to 5 minutes.
4. Remove to a bowl and wipe out the skillet.
5. Place 1 slice of bread, buttered-side down, into one side of the warm skillet.
6. Heat 1/2 tbsp. oil in the other side of the skillet.
7. Place mozzarella slices in the skillet and cook until soft, 1 to 2 minutes.
8. Place mozzarella slices on top of the bread in the skillet.
9. Repeat with the provolone, Asiago, and Fontina slices.
10. Add spinach mixture and tomato slices to the skillet, adding more oil if necessary, and cook until warm, 2 to 3 minutes.
11. Place spinach mixture on top of the cheese, followed by the tomatoes and the remaining slice of bread, buttered-side up. Flip the sandwich and cook until browned and cheese has melted, 5 to 10 minutes.

Eggplant Ricotta Grilled Cheese

Ingredients:

1 loaf Italian bread
2 medium tomatoes
1 large eggplant
1 tbsp. olive oil, or as needed
salt and ground black pepper to taste
1 cup ricotta cheese
8 leaves fresh basil
16 slices fontina cheese
2 tbsps. salted butter, or to taste

Directions:

1. Slice Italian bread info 8 thick slices.
2. Slice each tomato into 4 slices.
3. Remove some of the skin from the eggplant, leaving the rest of the skin on for a striped look.
4. Slice the eggplant into eight 1/2-inch rounds.
5. Heat olive oil in a skillet over medium heat.
6. Season eggplant with salt and pepper; cook until soft, about 5 minutes per side. Watch that it does not burn.
7. Remove to a plate and set aside.
8. Spread ricotta over 4 slices of bread.
9. Top each with 2 eggplant slices and 2 tomato slices.
10. Season tomatoes with salt and pepper.
11. Tear 2 basil leaves over each sandwich.
12. Add 4 slices of fontina cheese.
13. Spread butter over the remaining slices of bread and place over the cheese, buttered sides up.
14. Melt remaining butter in a large skillet over medium heat.
15. Add sandwiches to the skillet with the dry side down.
16. Cover with a piece of foil and place a heavy pan on top. Toast sandwiches for 3 to 4 minutes.
17. Flip over and cover again.
18. Cook until cheese is melted, 3 to 4 minutes more.

Pumpkin Bread Grilled Cheese

Ingredients:

1 cup milk
3/4 cup warm water
3 1/2 tbsps. honey
1 1/2 tbsps. instant yeast
6 1/2 cups bread flour
1/4 cup vegetable oil
3 tbsps. pumpkin puree
2 tsps. salt
1 tsp. cornmeal (Optional)

Grilled Cheese Sandwich Ingredients:

2 tbsps. mayonnaise
1/2 tsp. Dijon mustard, or to taste
2 slices Cheddar cheese
2 slices Gruyere cheese

Directions:

1. Combine milk, water, honey, and yeast in the bowl of an electric stand mixer.
2. Let sit for 10 minutes.
3. Pour flour, oil, pumpkin puree, and salt into the mixture.
4. Mix using a dough hook attachment until dough is soft, smooth, and tacky, 2 to 5 minutes.
5. Add more flour or water if needed.
6. Place dough on a lightly floured surface and knead by hand for 3 to 4 minutes.
7. Form into a ball and place into a large, greased bowl.
8. Cover with plastic wrap and let rise until doubled in size, 1 1/2 to 2 hours.
9. Preheat the oven to 495 degrees F (255 degrees C).
10. Place a large, cast iron Dutch oven into the oven to preheat.
11. Divide dough into 2 balls and flour lightly.
12. Place 1 ball back into the greased bowl, cover with plastic wrap, and save in the refrigerator for a later time.
13. Place remaining ball onto parchment paper that has been sprinkled with cornmeal.
14. Cover with plastic wrap and let rest for 30 minutes. Dust with flour and score.

Remove the preheated Dutch oven carefully from the oven and uncover.

Lift parchment paper with dough and place into the Dutch oven.

Trim any parchment paper that extends beyond the top.

Cover carefully with the hot lid.

Bake in the preheated oven for 20 minutes.

Remove lid and continue baking until golden, about 40 minutes more.

Remove from the oven and lift out bread carefully using the parchment paper.

Let cool on a wire rack for at least 30 minutes before slicing.

Make grilled cheese sandwiches once the loaf has cooled enough to slice.

Heat a skillet over medium heat.

Spread mayonnaise over one side of each bread slice.

Place bread mayonnaise-side down into the skillet.

Spread Dijon mustard on the other side.

Top with Cheddar cheese and Gruyere cheese slices.

Cook for 2 minutes; sandwich both halves together.

Cook until golden, 3 to 4 minutes per side.

Elvis' Grilled Cheese Sandwich

Ingredients:

2 slices bacon
1 tbsp. smooth peanut butter
2 slices soft white bread
1 slice American cheese
1 tbsp. butter, softened

Directions:

1. Place the bacon in a large, deep skillet, and cook over medium-high heat, turning occasionally, until evenly browned, about 10 minutes.
2. Drain the bacon slices on a paper towel-lined plate.
3. Spread peanut butter on a slice of white bread, and cover with cheese slice and bacon.
4. Top with the other piece of bread.
5. Spread butter on both sides of the sandwich, and pan-fry in a skillet over medium heat until the bread is golden brown and the cheese has melted, 2 to 3 minutes per side.
6. Serve hot.

Inside-Out Grilled Cheese Sandwich

Ingredients:

2 tbsps. butter, divided
2 slices white bread
1/2 cup shredded extra sharp Cheddar cheese, divided

Directions:

1. Melt 1 1/2 tbsps. butter in a nonstick skillet over medium-low heat.
2. Place bread slices in the skillet on top of the melted butter.
3. Spread about 1/4 cup Cheddar cheese on one slice of bread; place the other slice of bread, butter-side up, on top of the cheese.
4. Spread about 2 tbsps. of cheese on top of the sandwich.
5. Melt remaining 1/2 tbsp. butter in the skillet next to the sandwich.
6. Flip the sandwich onto the melted butter so that the cheese-side is facing down.
7. Spread remaining cheese on top of the sandwich.
8. Cook sandwich until cheese on the bottom is crispy and caramelized, 3 to 4 minutes.
9. Flip sandwich and cook until cheese is crispy and caramelized on the other side, another 3 to 4 minutes.

Bourbon Onions Grilled Cheese

Ingredients:

1 tbsp. olive oil
1 large red onion, halved, thinly sliced lengthwise
1 tbsp. brown sugar
1/4 tsp. each salt and freshly ground black pepper
1 tbsp. bourbon
1 1/2 tsp. plus 4 Tbsp unsalted butter, softened
3 cups of sharp cheddar and Gruyère, grated
8 (1/2-inch) slices crusty bread

Directions:

1. Heat oil in a large skillet over medium heat.
2. Add onion and cook 20 minutes, stirring frequently, until caramelized and very tender.
3. Stir in sugar, salt, and pepper.
4. Add bourbon, scraping up all brown bits in bottom of skillet.
5. Stir in 1 1/2 tsp. butter until melted; keep warm. (Makes about 1 cup.)
6. In a medium bowl, toss cheeses until well combined.
7. Divide evenly into 4 portions; press each into a disk-like patty to fit the size of the bread slices.
8. Spread 1/4 cup of the onion mixture on each of 4 slices of bread.
9. Top each with a cheese patty and another slice of bread.
10. Spread 1 1/2 tsp. of the butter on 1 side of each sandwich.
11. Heat a large nonstick skillet over medium-low heat.
12. Place 2 sandwiches, butter side down, in skillet.
13. Cook 3 to 4 minutes, until golden brown. While first side is cooking, spread 1 1/2 tsp. of the butter on other side of each sandwich. Turn sandwiches and cook 3 to 4 minutes, until second side is crispy and golden brown and cheese has melted.
14. Repeat with remaining 2 sandwiches.

Ham and Pimiento Grilled Cheese

Ingredients:

4 slice country or Pullman bread
1 tbsp. unsalted butter
4 oz. Cheddar
2 tbsp. cream cheese
1 tsp. Hot sauce
2 slice deli ham
1/4 cup sliced pimentos
2 scallions

Directions:

1. Brush one side of each slice of bread with butter or oil. Form sandwiches (buttered-side out) with the Cheddar, cream cheese, hot sauce, ham, pimientos, and scallions.
2. Heat a large nonstick skillet over low heat.
3. Cook the sandwiches, covered, until the bread is golden brown and crisp and the cheese has melted, 4 to 5 minutes per side.

Roast Beef French Onion Grilled Cheese

Ingredients:

1 tbsp. olive oil
1 small onion
1 tsp. thyme leaves
Kosher salt
pepper
4 slice rye bread
1 tbsp. melted unsalted butter or olive oil
1 tbsp. whole-grain mustard
2 oz. Gruyère cheese
2 slice roast beef

Directions:

1. Heat olive oil in a medium skillet over medium heat.
2. Add onion, season with 1/4 tsp. each salt and pepper, and cook, covered, stirring occasionally, for 12 minutes.
3. Reduce the heat to medium-low, stir in thyme leaves and cook, uncovered, stirring occasionally, until the onions are golden brown, 15 to 20 minutes more (add 1 tbsp. water to the skillet if the onions start sticking).
4. Brush one side of each slice of bread with butter or oil. Form sandwiches with the bread, whole-grain mustard, Gruyère cheese, roast beef, and the onion mixture.
5. Cook the sandwiches, covered, until the bread is golden brown and crisp and the cheese has melted, 4 to 5 minutes per side.

Pepperoni, Spinach and Mozzarella Grilled Cheese

Ingredients:

2 ciabatta rolls
1 tbsp. unsalted butter
2 tbsp. marinara sauce
4 oz. mozzarella
1 oz. pepperoni
1 cup baby arugula or spinach

Directions:

1. Brush the outsides of the rolls with butter or oil.
2. Form sandwiches (buttered-side out) with the marinara, mozzarella, pepperoni, and arugula.
3. Heat a large nonstick skillet over low heat.
4. Cook the sandwiches, covered, until the bread is golden brown and crisp and the cheese has melted, 4 to 5 minutes per side.

Monte Cristo Grilled Cheese Sandwich

Ingredients:

1/4 cup Fig Jam
1 tsp. fresh lemon juice
8 1/2"-thick slices sourdough bread
1/2 small red onion, thinly sliced
4 oz. thinly sliced ham or prosciutto (8 to 12 slices)
8 oz. fresh mozzarella, thinly sliced
1/4 cup whole milk
1 large egg
kosher salt
1/2 cup freshly grated Parmesan
Oil, for the baking sheet

Directions:

1. Place a rimmed baking sheet in the oven and heat to 425 degrees F (preheating the sheet helps the bread crisp).
2. Mix the jam and the lemon juice; spread onto 4 slices of bread.
3. Top with the onion, prosciutto, and mozzarella; sandwich with remaining slices of bread.
4. In a bowl, whisk together the milk, egg, and a pinch of salt.
5. Lightly brush the bread with the egg mixture, then sprinkle on the Parmesan (both sides of the sandwich should be fully coated in Parmesan).
6. Remove the baking sheet from the oven and drizzle with enough oil so the pan is coated (about 1 1/2 tbsp.), then place the sandwiches on top. Return to the oven and bake until golden brown, 8 to 10 minutes per side.

Thanksgiving Turkey Brie Grilled Cheese

Ingredients:

4 slices rye bread
4 tbsp. cranberry sauce
4 oz. sliced turkey
2 oz. brie, cut into pieces
4 pieces crisp bacon
1/2 cup baby spinach

Directions:

1. Place rye bread on a broiler-proof baking sheet.
2. Top 2 slices with cranberry sauce, sliced turkey, and Brie.
3. Broil until the cheese melts, about 1 minute.
4. Top the cheese with crisp bacon and baby spinach. Sandwich with the remaining bread slices.

Turkey Mozzarella Pesto Grilled Cheese

Ingredients:

1 bunch kale, leaves stripped and blanched
1 cup fresh basil leaves
1/2 cup extra-virgin olive oil, plus more for brushing bread
1/4 cup freshly grated Parmesan
1/4 cup walnuts
1 clove garlic
Kosher salt
1 loaf ciabatta or focaccia
1/2 lb. sliced turkey breast
1 large tomato, sliced
6 oz. mozzarella, sliced

Directions:

1. In the bowl of a food processor, combine kale, basil, and oil and pulse until combined.
2. Add Parmesan, walnuts, garlic, and salt and blend until combined.
3. Slather pesto on ciabatta and top with turkey, tomatoes, and mozzarella.
4. Brush bread with oil.
5. Cook in a panini press (or in a skillet over medium heat with a heavy pan on top to press it down) until golden and cheese is melty.

Raspberry Cheesecake French Toast Grilled Cheese

Ingredients:

1 cup milk
2 tbsps. vanilla extract
1 cup white sugar
2 tbsps. cinnamon
4 eggs, beaten
1 cup raspberry puree
4 oz. cream cheese, softened
1 loaf French bread, cut into 1 inch slices
Butter
Confectioners' sugar for dusting
Nutmeg, for topping

Directions:

1. In a bowl, whisk milk, vanilla, sugar, and cinnamon into the beaten eggs until well blended.
2. Set aside.
3. In a separate bowl, cream together raspberry puree and cream cheese until smooth.
4. Make 'sandwiches' by cutting each slice of bread in half and spreading raspberry-cheese mixture in the center, then top with the other half.
5. Melt butter over medium heat in a large skillet or griddle.
6. Dip bread into egg mixture, coating thoroughly.
7. Cook until well-browned on both sides, about 5 minutes. Dust with confectioners' sugar and nutmeg.
8. Serve immediately.

Southwestern Grilled Cheese

Ingredients:

2 slices sourdough bread
2 Tbsp. black bean salsa
3 slices roasted turkey breast
1 tsp. fresh cilantro
1 slice hot habanero cheese slice
1 tbsp. olive oil

Directions:

1. Heat panini grill.
2. Fill bread slices with salsa, turkey, cilantro and cheese.
3. Brush outside of sandwich with oil.
4. Grill 2 to 3 min. or until golden brown.

Cheddar and Chutney Grilled Cheese Sandwiches

Ingredients:

12 (1/4-inch-thick) slices bakery white bread
8 tbsp. (1 stick) unsalted butter, melted
1/2 cup plus 1 tbsp. mango chutney
2 cups extra-sharp white Cheddar, grated

Directions:

1. Lay 6 slices of bread on a work surface and brush evenly with 4 tbsps. butter. Turn the slices over and spread evenly with chutney.
2. Top with Cheddar, dividing evenly. Sandwich with remaining sliced bread. Brush tops generously with remaining 4 tbsps. butter.
3. Heat a panini press (see note).
4. Cook sandwiches according to manufacturer's directions, until bread is nicely browned on both sides and Cheddar is starting to melt.
5. Place sandwiches on a cutting board and cut in half diagonally.
6. Serve hot.

Sloppy Joe Grilled Cheese

Ingredients:

1 pound lean ground beef
1/2 medium onion, chopped
1/4 cup chopped green pepper
2/3 cup ketchup
1 1/2 tsps. Worcestershire sauce
1 tsp. ground mustard
1/2 tsp. garlic powder
1/8 tsp. cayenne pepper
8 slices Texas toast or hearty white bread
1 cup shredded cheddar cheese
4 tbsps. butter

Directions:

1. Add ground beef to a nonstick pan placed over medium heat.
2. Use a wooden spoon to break it apart as it cooks. As soon as you have it crumbled, add the onion and green pepper.
3. Cook until beef is no longer pink and onion and pepper is softened.
4. Add ketchup, dry mustard, garlic powder, Worcestershire sauce, and cayenne pepper.
5. Stir to combine well and cook over medium-low heat for 5 minutes.
6. Remove from heat.
7. For each sandwich, spread 1/4 cup cheese on top of one slice of bread.
8. Top with sloppy joe mixture.
9. Place second piece of bread on top.
10. Heat griddle or nonstick pan over medium heat.
11. Add 1/2 tbsp. butter, let it melt and place sandwich on top.
12. Cook until bottom is golden, lift sandwich with a spatula, place another 1/2 tbsp. of butter down, and flip sandwich over.
13. Cook until cheese is melted.

Grilled Cheese Dogs

Ingredients:

4 hot dogs
4 buns
8 slices bacon, cooked
1/2 cup shredded cheddar cheese
1/2 cup shredded Pepper Jack cheese
3 tbsps. butter, melted
1/2 tsp. garlic powder

Directions:

1. Heat a grill pan or griddle over medium-high heat.
2. Add garlic powder to melted butter.
3. Brush outsides and insides of buns with melted butter.
4. Cut a slit in hot dogs.
5. Place hot dogs and buns in grill pan and cook for about a minute on each side.
6. Place a hot dog in each bun, add 2 slices of bacon and 1/4 of the cheese to each one.
7. Close buns and press down with a spatula to flatten them some. Turn heat down to medium-low and cook until cheese is melted.

Pickle Bacon Grilled Cheese

Ingredients:

3 slice
cooked crispy, drain on paper towels
2 slice
bread of your choice
butter as needed
1 dill pickle sliced lengthwise
2 slice
Cheddar cheese
1 slice mozzarella cheese or 1 oz shredded

Directions:

1. Place a slice of bread on the counter, add a slice of Cheddar, then a layer of pickle slices, then the Mozzarella, then a layer of bacon, another slice of Cheddar, butter the other slice of bread and place that on top, butter side up.
2. Heat a non stick pan with about a tbsp. of butter, when melted and hot, pick the sandwich up and place in the pan.
3. Cook until the bottom is golden brown, then carefully flip the sandwich over and cook the other side until golden brown.
4. Remove to a plate, slice in half, enjoy.

Chicken Parm Grilled Cheese

Ingredients:

8 slices whole wheat bread
1 cup tomato sauce
8 oz. fresh mozzarella cheese, sliced

Chicken Parmesan Ingredients:

1 cup vegetable oil
3/4 cup Italian style breadcrumbs
1/4 cup freshly grated Parmesan
2 boneless, skinless chicken breasts, cut crosswise in half
1/2 cup all-purpose flour
2 large eggs, beaten

Directions:

1. Preheat a waffle iron to medium-high heat.
2. Lightly oil the top and bottom of the waffle iron or coat with nonstick spray.
3. Heat vegetable oil in a large skillet over medium high heat.
4. In a large bowl, combine breadcrumbs and Parmesan; set aside.
5. Working one at a time, dredge chicken in flour, dip into eggs, then dredge in breadcrumbs mixture, pressing to coat.
6. Add chicken to the skillet and cook until evenly golden and crispy, about 3-4 minutes.
7. Transfer to a paper towel-lined plate.
8. Working in batches, place bread slices into the waffle iron.
9. Top with chicken, tomato sauce, mozzarella and remaining bread slices.
10. Close gently and cook until golden brown and crisp, about 3-4 minutes.
11. Serve immediately.

Mac & Cheese Grilled Cheese

Ingredients:

4 slices sourdough or other dense bread
8 slices American cheese or cheddar cheese
2 tbsps. butter
1 1/2 cups leftover macaroni and cheese

Directions:

1. Over medium heat, warm 3/4 cup of mac & cheese In a small nonstick skillet. Once warm (about 3-4 minutes), shape mac & cheese into a square about the size of the bread and top with 2 slices of cheese. Turn off heat.
2. Butter 2 slices of bread and place both slices butter side down in another skillet over medium heat.
3. Top one of the bread slices with 2 slices cheese.
4. When lightly browned turn off heat.
5. Use spatula to transfer mac & cheese rectangle onto cheese covered bread in the skillet.
6. Cover with the other bread slice, toasted side up.
7. Gently press together with spatula and transfer to a plate.
8. Serve immediately.

Pizza Grilled Cheese

Ingredients:

1 tbsp. unsalted butter
4 slices Bread
4 slices mozzarella cheese, 1/8-inch thick
18 slices pepperoni cooked in microwave for 20 seconds and grease dabbed off
For the garlic butter
3 tbsp. unsalted butter
1/4 tsp. fresh or dried parsley
1/4 tsp. Italian seasoning
1/4 tsp. garlic powder
1/8 tsp. salt

Directions:

1. In a medium skillet set over medium-low heat, add the butter and melt.
2. Place two pieces of toast side by side.
3. To each slice of bread, add a slice of mozzarella, 9 pepperoni, and another slice of mozzarella.
4. Place remaining slices of bread on top.
5. Cook on each side for about 3 minutes or until the cheese is melty.
6. Meanwhile, make the garlic butter.
7. In a small microwave safe bowl, add the butter.
8. Heat until melted.
9. Stir in parsley, Italian seasoning, garlic powder, and salt.
10. Using a pastry brush, brush on both sides of grilled cheese.
11. Cook on each side for 30 seconds.
12. Remove, sprinkle with parmesan cheese and dip in your favorite marinara, if desired.

Mexican Fajita Grilled Cheese

Ingredients:

1/2 large red onion, sliced
3 bell peppers, sliced
1 medium zucchini, thinly sliced or ribboned with a peeler
2 tbsp olive oil
1 tsp minced garlic
1 tsp coarse sea salt
1/4 tsp black pepper
1/2 tsp cumin powder
Butter
8 slices hearty wheat or white bread
1/4 cup Cilantro Parsley Chimichurri Sauce
8 slices mozzarella cheese

Directions:

1. Heat olive oil in large skillet over medium-high heat.
2. Add in onions and garlic. Sauté until fragrant, about 1 minute.
3. Add in bell peppers, zucchini, cumin powder, salt and black pepper.
4. Cook until softened, about 10 min.
5. Remove from heat.
6. Then, grab one slice of bread and butter one side.
7. Place the bread, buttered-side down, on a flat griddle pan or skillet.
8. Layer with 1 tbsp chimichurri sauce, 2 slices mozzarella cheese (about 2 oz.) and 3/4 cup fajita veggies.
9. Top with another slice of bread and butter the outside.
10. Heat skillet on medium heat.
11. Flip grilled cheese when mozzarella starts to melt.
12. Cook for another 2 to 4 minutes.
13. Slice in halve.
14. Repeat steps 4 through 11 to make the remaining grilled cheese sandwiches.

Spinach and Artichoke Dip Grilled Cheese

Ingredients:

1 tsp. of olive oil
1 cup fresh baby spinach, packed
1/4 cup jarred artichokes, chopped
1 garlic clove, peeled and minced
Crushed red pepper
Worcestershire sauce
Salt
2 oz. softened cream cheese
3 tbsp. finely shredded parmesan
1 cup finely shredded mozzarella
4 slices of brioche, sourdough or white bread

Directions:

1. In a medium saucepan, set over medium heat, warm the olive oil.
2. Add the spinach and cook until mostly wilted.
3. Add the artichokes, garlic, pinch crushed red pepper, dash Worcestershire sauce and a few pinches of salt.
4. Cook for 1 to 2 minutes, until artichokes are warm.
5. Transfer to bowl.
6. Set aside.
7. In a small bowl, mix together the cream cheese, with a dash of Worcestershire, pinch of crushed red pepper and parmesan.
8. To assemble, add a few swipes of the cream mixture to one slice of bread.
9. Top with a handful of mozzarella, the artichoke and spinach mixture and then top with the second slice of bread.
10. Repeat with the second grilled cheese. To a medium saucepan, melt 1 tbsp. of butter.
11. When melted add the grilled cheese and cook for 1 to 2 minutes, covering immediately, and then flipping.
12. Cook on the opposite side for an additional minute, until the cheese is oozing out the sides.
13. Repeat the cooking process with the remaining grilled cheese.

Fried Green Tomato Grilled Cheese

Ingredients:

1/2 cup all purpose flour
1 cup buttermilk
1/2 cup cornmeal
1/2 cup bread crumbs
1 tsp. kosher salt
1/2 tsp. freshly ground black pepper
1/4 tsp. cayenne
2-3 green tomatoes sliced into 3/8 inch slices, discard the bottoms and tops
2-3 cups vegetable oil
4 slices English muffin bread or other white bread
3-4 tbsps. butter at room temperature
8 oz. pepper jack cheese

Directions:

1. Scoop the flour onto a plate or large bowl.
2. Pour the buttermilk into a bowl.
3. Mix the cornmeal, bread crumbs, kosher salt, black pepper and cayenne on another plate or large bowl.
4. Dip a tomato slice into the flour, tossing so both sides and all of the edges are coated.
5. Dip in the buttermilk then dredge in the cornmeal bread crumb mixture, gently patting both sides so the coating adheres.
6. Place on a wire rack and continue with the rest of the tomatoes.
7. Pour enough vegetable oil into a large skillet or cast iron pan to fill it about 1/2 inch from the bottom.
8. Heat to medium high until the oil is about 350 degrees F.
9. Fry the tomatoes in batches, about 3-4 at a time, flipping once so both sides are lightly browned.
10. Drain the tomatoes on another wire rack that's been set over paper towels.
11. Repeat for the rest of the tomatoes.
12. Spread 1/2 tbsp. of butter on one side of each slice of the bread, then stack buttered sides together.

13. Cut the Monterey jack into thin slices and layer on the bottom slice of the sandwich, then layer 2-3 tomato slices (cut the tomatoes if needed to fit the bread—then layer more cheese slices on top.
14. Place the bread buttered side down in a fry pan over medium heat.
15. Cover with a lid and let cook for 3-4 minutes or until golden.
16. Reduce the heat to medium-low and flip sandwich to the other side and cook for 2-3 minutes or until bread is toasty golden and cheese has melted.
17. The second side will cook faster than the first so watch carefully.
18. Cut in half and enjoy hot.

Brussels Sprouts Grilled Cheese

Ingredients:

4 tsps. extra-virgin olive oil
1 small onion, finely sliced
Kosher salt and freshly ground black pepper
1 1/2 cups finely shredded brussels sprouts (about 6 oz.)
4 slices hearty sourdough or French bread
6 oz. sharp cheddar cheese, sliced
3 tbsps. unsalted butter

Directions:

1. Heat 2 tsps. olive oil in a medium cast iron pan or skillet over medium heat until shimmering.
2. Add onions, season with salt and pepper, and cook, stirring frequently, until golden brown, 15 to 20 minutes.
3. Transfer to a bowl and wipe out skillet.
4. Return skillet to high heat and add remaining 2 tsps. oil.
5. Heat until lightly smoking.
6. Add brussels sprouts, season with salt and pepper, and cook, tossing and stirring occasionally, until wilted and lightly charred, about 2 minutes.
7. Transfer to bowl and wipe out skillet.
8. Spread onions and sprouts over one side of two slices of bread.
9. Top with cheddar cheese and remaining two slices of bread.
10. Melt 1 1/2 tbsps. butter in same skillet over medium-low heat. Swirl to coat pan.
11. Add sandwiches.
12. Place a skillet on top of them and press down gently.
13. Cook, turning pan and moving sandwiches occasionally until well browned on first side, about 4 minutes.
14. Remove from skillet with a flexible metal spatula.
15. Melt remaining 1 1/2 tbsps. butter.
16. Return sandwiches to skillet uncooked-side-down and continue cooking, turning pan and moving sandwiches occasionally until well browned and cheese is melted, about 4 minutes longer.
17. Serve immediately.

Bagel Grilled Cheese

Ingredients:

1 split bagel
mayonnaise
spicy mustard
2 slices muenster
2 slices salami
1 tbsp. salted butter plus more if needed

Directions:

1. Spread a split bagel with mayonnaise and spicy mustard.
2. Sandwich with 1 slice muenster, 2 slices salami and another slice of muenster.
3. Heat butter in a cast-iron or nonstick skillet over medium-low heat.
4. Cook sandwich, flipping once, until golden, pressing to flatten.

Cajun Grilled Cheese

Ingredients:

2 slices country white bread
2 slices provolone
1 tbsp. salted butter plus more if needed
1 pinch of Cajun seasoning

Directions:

1. Sandwich 2 slices country white bread with 2 slices provolone.
2. Heat butter in a cast-iron or nonstick skillet over medium-low heat.
3. Sprinkle with Cajun seasoning.
4. Cook sandwich, flipping once, until golden, pressing to flatten.

Brie and Marmalade Grilled Cheese

Ingredients:

2 slices cinnamon-raisin bread
Orange marmalade
2 slices brie (remove the rind)
1 tbsp. salted butter plus more if needed

Directions:

1. Spread bread with orange marmalade.
2. Sandwich with brie.
3. Heat butter in a cast-iron or nonstick skillet over medium-low heat.
4. Cook sandwich, flipping once, until golden.

Kimchi Grilled Cheese

Ingredients:

2 tbsps. canola oil
8 (1-oz.) whole-wheat bread slices
3 oz. thinly sliced fresh mozzarella cheese
1 1/2 oz. (1/3 cup) shredded Monterey Jack cheese
2 tbsps. chopped kimchi

Directions:

1. Brush canola oil evenly over 1 side of whole-wheat bread slices.
2. Arrange 4 bread slices, oiled side down, on a work surface.
3. Divide thinly sliced fresh mozzarella cheese and shredded Monterey Jack cheese evenly among arranged bread slices.
4. Top each with 2 tbsps. chopped kimchi and 1 bread slice, oiled side up.
5. Cook sandwiches in a large nonstick skillet over medium-high until toasted and cheese is melted, about 3 minutes on each side.

Vermont Grilled Cheese

Ingredients:

1 tbsp. salted butter
4 slices whole wheat bread
4 oz. sharp cheddar, sliced
6 slices applewood smoked bacon, cooked until crisp
2 tsps. maple syrup

Directions:

1. Melt butter in large skillet over medium-low heat.
2. Top two bread slices with cheese and bacon.
3. Drizzle with maple syrup and press remaining bread slices on top.
4. Transfer to skillet and cook slowly until golden on underside, reducing heat if needed.
5. Turn and cook until sandwiches are golden on second side and cheese is melted.

California Grilled Cheese

Ingredients:

1 tbsp. Salted Butter
4 slices sourdough bread
4 oz. Pepper Jack, sliced
6 slices tomato
1/2 avocado, sliced

Directions:

1. Melt butter in large skillet over medium-low heat.
2. TOP two bread slices with cheese, tomato and avocado.
3. Place remaining bread slices on top.
4. Transfer to skillet and cook slowly until golden on underside, reducing heat if needed.
5. Turn and cook until sandwiches are golden on second side and cheese is melted.

Anchovy Grilled Cheese

Ingredients:

2 anchovy filets, finely chopped or 1 tsp. anchovy paste
4 tsps. mayonnaise
4 slices multigrain bread
2 oz. Garlic Herb Cheddar, shredded (about 1/2 cup)
4 slices ripe slicing tomato
1 tbsp. Unsalted Butter, cut in half

Directions:

1. Mix anchovy and mayonnaise in a small dish.
2. Lay bread slices on work surface.
3. Spread anchovy aioli on the bread.
4. Divide cheddar between two of the slices.
5. Top with tomato and the remaining two slices of bread.
6. Heat half the butter in a large non-stick over medium heat.
7. When butter is melted, arrange two of the sandwiches in the skillet.
8. Cook until browned on the bottom, 4 to 4 minutes.
9. Add the second half of the butter to the skillet and carefully flip sandwiches over, adjusting heat as necessary to prevent browning.
10. Cook until the cheese is melted and the bottoms are browned, 3 to 5 minutes longer.
11. Cut in half to serve.

Poblano Grilled Cheese Sandwiches

Ingredients:

2 poblano peppers
1/2 avocado
1 tsp. freshly squeezed lime juice, or to taste
1/8 tsp. salt
2 tbsps. Unsalted Butter, softened
4 slices large bread
1/2 cup Sharp Cheddar, shredded

Directions:

1. Arrange oven rack in upper third of the oven.
2. Preheat broiler to high heat.
3. Line a baking sheet with aluminum foil.
4. Place poblanos on the prepared sheet and broil, turning occasionally, until the skin is blackened, blistered and charred on all sides, about 10 minutes.
5. Carefully transfer the peppers to a bowl, cover and set aside to cool.
6. Mash avocado in a small bowl with the lime and salt to taste.
7. Spread butter over one side of each slice of bread.
8. Turn bread over and spread avocado mixture on two slices of the bread.
9. Divide cheddar between the other two slices of bread.
10. Peel the charred skin off when peppers are cool enough to handle.
11. Remove stems and seeds and cut the peppers in half.
12. Lay the pepper halves over the cheese and top with the avocado smeared halves.
13. Lay the assembled sandwiches in a large skillet and place over medium-low heat, cook until golden on the outside and cheese is melted on the inside, 3 to 5 minutes per side.
14. Cut in half to serve.

About the Author

Laura Sommers is **The Recipe Lady!**

She lives on a small farm in Baltimore County, Maryland and has a passion for food. She has taken cooking classes in Memphis, New Orleans and Washington DC. She has been a taste tester for a large spice company in Baltimore and written food reviews for several local papers. She loves writing cookbooks with the most delicious recipes to share her knowledge and love of cooking with the world.

Follow her on Pinterest:

http://pinterest.com/therecipelady1

Visit the Recipe Lady's blog for even more great recipes:

http://the-recipe-lady.blogspot.com/

Visit her Amazon Author Page to see her latest books:

amazon.com/author/laurasommers

Follow the Recipe Lady on Facebook:

https://www.facebook.com/therecipegirl

Follow her on Twitter:

https://twitter.com/TheRecipeLady1

Please take a moment to leave a review for this book. It really helps me out as well as my family. I appreciate every reader and I work hard to bring you the best cookbooks that I can at the most reasonable price. Thank you!

Other Books by Laura Sommers

Irish Recipes for St. Patrick's Day

Traditional Vermont Recipes

Traditional Memphis Recipes

Maryland Chesapeake Bay Blue Crab Cookbook

Mussels Cookbook

Maryland Chesapeake Bay Blue Crab Cookbook

Salmon Cookbook

Scallop Recipes

Cool Amazon Merch

I Love Jesus Tee Shirt

Jesus Disco Tee Shirt

Smiley Face Tshirt

Slava Ukraini Glory To Ukraine Support Ukrainian Flag T-Shirt

I Stand with Ukraine Tshirt

Cougar Bait Halloween Tshirt - Younger Man Older Woman Here Kitty Kitty

Hey All You Cool Cats and Kittens Funny Carol Baskin Halloween Tshirt

Hello My Name is Karen Funny Halloween Tshirt

Crabcakes and Football That's What Maryland Does

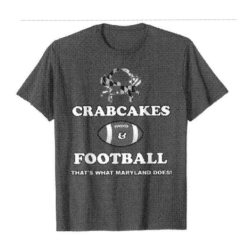

Maryland Girl Tshirt - All Shirts available in other colors

Pardon My Frenchie French Bulldog Lover Tshirt

Ready to Attack First Grade Shark Back to School

Ready to Attack First Grade Tshirt